SYMPATHY LOOPHOLE

SYMPATHY LOOPHOLE

JAIME FORSYTHE

Mansfield Press

a stuart ross book

Printed in Canada

Library and Archives Canada Cataloguing in Publication

Forsythe, Jaime, 1980-
Sympathy loophole / Jaime Forsythe.

Poems.
ISBN 978-1-894469-74-6

I. Title.

PS8611.O7728S96 2012 C811'.6 C2012-900887-7

Editor for the press: Stuart Ross
Publisher: Denis De Klerck
Typesetting: Stuart Ross
Author photo & cover design: Paul Hammond

The publication of *Sympathy Loophole* has been generously supported by the Canada Council for the Arts and the Ontario Arts Council.

Canada Council for the Arts Conseil des Arts du Canada
ONTARIO ARTS COUNCIL CONSEIL DES ARTS DE L'ONTARIO

Mansfield Press Inc.
25 Mansfield Avenue, Toronto, Ontario, Canada M6J 2A9
Publisher: Denis De Klerck
www.mansfieldpress.net

for my parents

CONTENTS

DOMESTIC MYSTERY

We hired a private investigator to locate the plants
in our apartment. She clicked in circles, magnifying
glass in one hand, pyjama-stuffed briefcase
in the other. Wet rings shone on our shelves. This
is the toughest job I've had yet, she said, tweezing
a yellow leaf from between two cushions. We were
helpless, popping ice cubes from the tray. A single
firework sighed into the night.

FORTUNE

You will see a mountain. You will uncover a code
at the checkout. Be alert for strange dogs
in your basement and very clean windows.
If you encounter a baby carriage, keep
walking. If you trip on a phoneme outside
of your native language, wrestle with it until it lies
flat. If awoken at five by sidewalk construction,
slide into a second dream. When the shape-shifters
knock, let them in. When dread and forgotten names
join hands, hold your breath. Each time you round
a corner in search of a lavatory, another flight
of stairs will appear. You won't know the structure
of the aircraft you're in. Relief is close at hand.

REAL-LIFE PHRASES IN EVERYDAY ENGLISH

Heather concluded the fugue with a tympani solo.

Claire gave a speech in her own language, with gestures.

George dreamt of the apothecary where his whims were once met.

Felicia's test results revealed that she did not have typhoid.

Henry argued that the platypus could be classified only as a hoax.

Gloria ordered smoked eel, visited a castle, and appeared onstage.

Alan was a dentist and a father, but mostly a dentist.

Errol imagined his teeth shaking free, white scattered in the wheat.

Naomi's children began to say things she did not understand.

Susanne peeled oranges while watching the war on television.

Anne adopted a name she would never again have to repeat.

FORMER GIRL GUIDE GOES CAMPING

I spelled *Cassiopeia* to earn
the astronomy badge, carpooled
to the planetarium. Concentric circles of blue
dresses. Phoebe ring, falling
star, meteorite. A girl's right
hand on my left armrest. My gaze strung
between the Milky Way and the reef
knot moving at her throat.

Ten years later, you inherit
an Oldsmobile. Our first-aid kit a box
of toothpicks. You roll fast cigarettes
on the divided highway.
To pitch or continue, sink our corners
into tilting earth or keep
aiming for a spot that's faultless.

A bedroom mock-up. A forest
diorama. You uncover the adventure
badge stitched to my hip, skin
healing over thread. Belt buckles
that would bring us to the bottom
of the sea. I learned CPR by breathing
into a Styrofoam head, its mouth
wiped with alcohol between girls.

We identify nothing, give nothing
its name. Guess at what's poison, which
stars are stars. I remember fire
starters of sawdust, wax, egg cartons,
when I used my resources
wisely. We neglect to repel insects.

Collect twist ties and hollow bottles.
Collapse the tent's tendons, what gives
it shape, wear another layer.
The ground a bowl. Our bitten
ankles. We're equally close
to two different towns.

Over and over, I convince myself
I want only one thing.

CONTORTIONS

Lessons in how to bend, how
to slot a body into the best
hiding spot, how to pretzel
for the prize, to hula hoop
away the disappointment.

On the days our skin was brass,
what we would do for two wheels,
or even one. The skid of gravel
on knees. The snails that formed
along your arms in the dark.

I experience a private perceptual
event at the snack bar. Children
with this disease are drawn
to musical instruments.
They send their breath
down canals of clarinets,
while marching, yodelling, and sipping
glasses of water. A new reed tastes
like a tree. The ball is headed
for the favourite's glove.
A flock of cameras
rise in unison.

ROMANCE

That year, we all had waitressing jobs
and stalkers.
Sore teeth and short answers.
Bruised hips and heavy pockets.
Good deadbolts and lucid dreams.
Giggled over the peeping Tom problem
on Maynard Street. A flipped lapel a follower.
A cellophaned flower delivered in March
during the spare change of a double shift.
He trailed slush past the good-luck
bowls of salt in the doorway, left
with free chopsticks. Whispered about a six-pack
stashed in the cemetery.

Don't burn those onions.
Have I failed you lately?
Stories of their youth:
ping-pong champs with prize collies.

We knew the importance of lighting,
the knee-length minimum. But also:
write down their lines to share
over spiked tea. You could fill a book.
We'll laugh even more about this when we're old
and no one's following us home.

TO DO

Fashion a camera obscura to project the tides.
Fill a foggy night with gloves and persimmons.
Play a game of violence in a cold parlour.
Convince conjoined twins to cast secret ballots.
Be discreet, confident, alluring, and kind.
Pick out a tombstone on a Sunday drive.

SMALL TOWN

You fold in upon yourself. Pillowcases
as envelopes, notes slipped in with
the feathers. Swirl of unwashed sheets, dirt
road out the window. Red flag flipped
like even the mailbox is hitching a ride
out of here. Seals licked shut. The wasp speaks
to wake us: a wing rub, a one-note drone.

Looseleaf fan, accordion pleats, floor-length
floral. Paintbrush tips of a niece's braids
caught in the clothesline ghosts, games
of tag startling intimate fabrics.
Inchworms drip from doubled-up hems.

The wasp drowns in your little bit of courage,
finger of rum from the night before.
Closet empty except for a paperback
and a striped tie. You dress for the funeral.
Later, I ease buttons through buttonholes.
The program flutters away from your chest.

You fold in upon yourself as the milk expires
and the news repeats. The house next door
was demolished slowly, nail by nail,
frequent smoke breaks. Now all that remains—
a heap of cast-iron radiators, the heat gone
from them. Heavy what gets left behind.

STRANGER AT THE WAKE

I do not wish to inconvenience
with my presence. If I could just sit
awhile, by the gilded plate,
trail my hand over polished
cedar, drift into lack
of recognition. If I drape a grey
pashmina, bring my own flask, keep
the music low. Smile sad and palm
tissues, mouth a hymn
swirled with whiskey
while grief elapses against stiff petals
and shushed kids. As I steal into
this loophole, I can almost feel it.
How I long to be exhausted.

STEPS THE SIZE OF SEEDS

Apologies plucked from stale birdbaths.
A wedding band tapped on a dash.
The unused lot, car doors
never denting. Every second space.
I shrank two inches last year.
Inappropriate comments in the vestibule.
A queue for the communal phone.
I tried to fix things with quickbreads.
I left that version in the bathroom
big enough for ten wheelchairs.
He peeled back the cotton to find
the old me. There were thick file folders,
neon tabs marking the seasons.
All I could write were bullets,
salient rebuttals. They sent
me home, but I had no home,
only a box inside a box. I pilfered
furniture from renounced dollhouses,
drawers that really opened, books
that didn't, piano keys painted on.
I patronized the tiny library, filled
my sacks at the mini-mart, took little
photographs. Everything fit perfectly.
Every month, I crossed one giant
square of sidewalk off my growing list.

OREGANO DRIP

They nourished him during his final days
in the wholesome wing. Wonder spice flecked
his veins, flavoured the sweat his collarbone
collected, tinted his complexion moss. Yet
we worried. Such small circumferences.
IV a worm. We said *Turn*
it up, turn it up, rain it over him
from bulk bags, hope his pores will open,
a million mouths gulping. Green
filled the air, like confetti, like
something dried and made smaller.

I LOST MY TRAIN

Someone drew me a picture
of my house. The doorbell rang,
but it was only a wisp of salt fog,
ghosting by. A surname
was stencilled on each boxcar.
I lost my train. For a man
who likes a taste of the wet,
ten rooms is too many.
I've got one miracle for you:
an ounce can be heaven.
Racing the whistle is no longer
brave; those tracks
haven't held freight
for years.

LAVENDER PULSE

He was in a home, had soft bones, paused
for days between thoughts, but knew when
every one of us was born. All those phone calls,
triple ring of a rural party line as the entire block
eavesdropped. Never knew privacy. Walls
thinned to curtains; his skin became transparent.
Blow-ups of his organs; amplified tune of his heart.
The nurse was a man. The nurse was his son, and his
grandson, and his best friend from high school.
The nurse snuck him chocolate, leaked lavender
oil from a pocket vial over his wrists, and said *Rest.*

SHARK IN A JAR

FD & C Blue No. 1 plus formaldehyde
looks just like the Atlantic. Face-first
in sealed aqua, banana-shaped. Memories
of boardwalk daiquiris, the mosaic
of his mother's shed teeth glittering
from a sandbar. His smile a slit throat.

He thought there would be others—
pickled playmates. Perhaps stunted
threats: scorpion in a jar, tarantula in a jar.
Or babies kept cute forever: flamingo in a jar,
manatee in a jar. Or freaks, saved from
sideshow life: tiniest girl in the world in a jar.
They'd float towards one another, finger to fin.

But he's perched between mantle knickknacks.
Bust of Freud, kissing angels, homemade
dreamcatcher. He dreams of dunes,
tapas and jazz, fusion cuisine, the cheerful
tourist trolley, the useless whistles that swung
against well-oiled chests of lifeguards.
The jewelled Ferris wheel after dark. Here,
houseguests rock his mini-tank from side
to side, as if they could wake him, as if
he were precious.

SATURDAY AFTERNOON COLLISION

On one side of the street, a juror checks her watch.
On the other, a truck reels into a tollbooth,
but no one is hurt. Tokens settle into potholes.
Every person who runs past us
is someone I used to know.
We opt for the cinema. Our tickets instruct,
Do not laugh and do not stop,
our fortunes in the portions ripped away.
To stay here forever would be a crime.
But what you love is everything giant
and loud, the space between rumble
and hush, the burst of feathers,
the applause at our backs.

BAKERY TALE

They escape through the woods to punch
in before dawn, from brick houses mortared
with boiled icing. They snap branches, hold
tinderboxes close, rub their raccoon eyes,
earplugs jammed into pockets of regulation
black pants. They leave trails: locks of hair, curled
bus transfers, chewed gum. They breathe silver

in the walk-in freezer. Danishes drained of their gold,
bloodless croissants plumped in the oven. Both hands
stamped, they cry over the radio; they know what goes
into those songs. The ratio of flours, the dates in place
of sugar, the pummelled butter, the lies. They tighten

their aprons, shudder slumped over the bread
slicer, racket of dry convulsions. Best brioche
in the city. Dogs with eyes large as teacups
stare from the patio. At night they scrape darkness
from urns, change into something better
in the back room, shoulder blades brushing the furnace.
They fasten their capes, extinguish the signs.
They retrace their steps.

MOTHER AND DAUGHTER

Hard to tell one
from the other.
Teapot bodies tip to pull
weeds, water favourite
perennials, daphne and phlox.
Bellies steep porch cola, stunned
by a bleached noon sky. Plastic
seats, saliva necklace. They gather
corner scenes, know each cop's nickname.

One's face crumples
less. One's almost bald. Lost
hair becomes soil,
compost, a distant nest.
One does more work:
the bringing and wiping. The pulling.
She borrows the boy's mower.
Its shudder numbs her hands,
sucks up the radio's Top 10.

Lunch under the umbrella,
unsteady lawn. Iceberg,
radish, pickle, and ham. Peach
t-shirt with a mustard stripe.
Greased napkins crushed, then
slowly unfurling.
Flamingoes' legs a blur.

ATTENTION

Apartment security-cam channel and cold ramen
He watches it like a soap, like the game
No one else aware of the feed, never a direct stare
He begins to feel he's been hired, anxious
if he misses too many comings, goings
Slack faces float over the threshold, no audio
Hours of the elevator's extinguished buttons
Poor resolution, poor contrast, but people have caught
ghosts on these things, it's true, vandals, loiterers,
even mail theft, a federal offense, worth reporting
He will be the sole eyewitness if anything ever happens
In the laundry room, the front loader doors are portholes
on a ship, his crouch reflected in the foam
Sees a sweater he knows, a flinching stance
In here they are all strange, no fingerprints or iris patterns
to be sure, left with shifting outfits and the latest hairstyles,
holding their damp sweatpants and thongs
Him, they don't worry about, no one else
is paying any attention at all

SNOWBANK SOMNAMBULIST

Drone of numbers in a white alley, calling
just to hear the low flutter, the flicker of
a hang-up. A phone, or a succession of phones.
Pitted along the gleaming street, various points
of contact. Listen for my bone-conducted
signal. The flour in my eyes
makes everything thick.
All protocol has altered since my last sleepwalk.
Every lock clicked shut. Outside a bar
with no sign, a bike I know
is chained to a pipe, its spokes glass,
its basket full of roses, its red bell missing.

BBQ

Dad seems to be having a problem
with the watermelon, but the bunting
is fantastic. A loud print, antennae
in the picture window, silverware
asleep in a teal kitchen. Masked children
squat in ditches, armed with swizzle sticks
and neon swords. Paste in an elbow crook,
residue of protection from the elements.
A hot ankle props open an aluminum door
to make way for a platter. An earring
in the grass. The singing begins.

FLIGHT

The seed of the idea in the warnings. What they could and could not make themselves do. At school they etherized *drosophila melanogaster*, diagnosed the bodies under microscopes. Dark-bellied dew lovers. With soft paintbrushes, they sorted. White-eyed, sepia-eyed, wildtype. After school and before supper, the hours where they didn't quite exist. Flies followed them, clung to the untouched bananas in their backpacks. Intimate friends. Feet off the chesterfield. What they could and could not stop themselves from doing. No need to be playing on that bridge. The adults still called it playing. You want to swim, you swim at the lake. Sleepy cows. No need to be jumping off that bridge into that river. Everything they needed. Double yolks and satellite dishes. Jell-O for dessert. He was fifteen. That boy who drowned, before you were born. He was twelve. The milkman found his body. He was six. One spring. He froze. They stripped down: freckles, scars, birthmarks. Microscopic. The turquoise river, brown if drawn up in cupped palms. The naked eye. Pretending not to look. Shiny milk trucks. White foam of the waterfall in the distance. They were numb to stories meant to scare. They stood in a line and smelled burning. Crimson afternoon. Tomatoes cooked down to a sauce. Pickles and moonshine. The steel guardrail. Feet curled over rock. Cigarettes from the reserve. The first one went over and six throats closed, then cheered. His slicked head, gasping, laughing. Rattle of a spraypaint can. We were here. One after another, crooked shapes in the sky. Cannonball. Bottle toke. The drowned boy didn't jump, was the difference. He just walked right in off the bank. Flipped stories. Thrilling plummet, impossible to remember properly afterwards. Black water. Don't be late. The second it takes to decide.

TESTS

Make-up exam in a room at high altitude,
she fills bubbles with a lead tip. Daydreams
of yesterday, when she wore a sheet
like a Hollywood gown. The floating
invigilator allocates limp booklets.
The windows bolted, blue flies and soft tar,
she crafts second guesses, bullies
answers from her brain. Scratches with pencil
at the phantom crepe on her belly, after
that stirrupped hour on a livid table. State
your assumptions. Tests pile until they lean.
The sign above the fire alarm says *Remain
Calm*, so she does.

INTRUDER

He wakes just as the dark film outdoors
is starting to split. Soft depressions
in the meadow. He knows a stranger
stands in the cottage, flushed
temple pressed to the medicine
cabinet, undecided.

The day before, the neighbour, in trunks,
trained a metal detector on the beach,
over crumbs, snapped limbs of plastic
men, shadows, wrappers, claws, cellophane,
string, tacks. And then, two quick beeps.

Thud of a docked paddle boat, bottles
rolling in scum. Skeptical geese.
He remembers his dream, the one
that warned him to watch the spotlit weeds,
to lie down in the required field.

Wicker trash basket of unopened mail.
Sugar whispers out of its bag. Muffled collisions
of dishes underwater, two lukewarm hands, wrists
cuffed in soap. A hiccupping needle:
I only   I only   I only

He hears bootsteps decrescendo, thinks,
This room is perfectly safe.

DAY JOB

It's not a gorilla. It's a man
in a gorilla suit. Maybe his true
loves are telescopes, lawn furniture,
or the lottery. Unanticipated risks
of contract employment include
velcro chafe, heat stroke, faux fur
allergy. A dog nods at him, wants to talk
shop. A shuffle around the circus perimeter
reveals nothing unusual.

Eyeholes erase the shades
between fear and delight. He lunges,
mistakes a balloon for a human
head, embraces a zebra. A real one. They are one
two-headed creature who is not faxing invoices
or filing files. The trampolinist somersaults,
elastic returning her to the sky,
again and again and again.

GAMES

I stepped into a statue
to see if I would fit, tilted
my head and raised my arms,
shouldered a musket, held still hoping
no one would notice my blinks.
I felt my skin harden and turn dull
bronze, standing above a plaque
bearing my name that some paused
to read on their way to the Mexican
restaurant where you can order
a burrito the size of a baby, and if
you finish every bite win a t-shirt,
say *cheese* with the wait staff.
Meanwhile I was frozen outside,
no longer trembling or wishing
I had someplace interesting to be.

AUDIT

You'll want to leave space
for careful records. The closest cubby
will do. Preferably, a nook with give.
A time will come when you'll be asked
to divulge the absent data,
the reluctant subject,
the midnights that didn't count
towards the stark graph we see today,
blooming away in their own dark cupboards.
Expect that outliers will murmur
amongst themselves. A figure must enter
each cell before fading.

FIVE MINUTES

The lake is a river, the path
a dead end. Arms crossed,
we blow smoke as ice settles
behind us, crackle and ache.
Taste of citrus and snow,
the crumble of dry brush,
a question that hovers. I don't know
how much longer I can wait.

MORNING AFTER

Free boxes from yesterday's yard sales soften, jammed
with maps and kites. Steam and wet benches by the corner
restaurant, a huddle of shy mushrooms. Hoods circle
for seats, pretend not to eavesdrop on fights over zippers
and thirst. Hands shake over hangman, an arrow drawn
on a palm and a strong lifeline. You could delay a whole
month, a year. Too nearsighted to read the chalkboard,
to spell the special. She doesn't reply because she's counting.
Steampunk pileup at the cream. Panic in reliving last night's
red sky, warm wind that coaxed bikes to the wrong side
of the road, the rising smoke that never got any closer
or farther away. A cat in a cage of branches. The fire
department said, *Call back when something starts burning.*

A VENTRILOQUIST, ON WHAT HIS DUMMY IS LIKE

He's a bit of a ladies' man. *Hey, ladies.*
He can't help himself.
He hates the box. It's dark.
I shimmy my hand into him
and he yelps. Comes alive to revel
in my flaws, fluent even
in the labial consonants:
You're bald, boring, poor.
My face doesn't move.
He travels carry-on, fits
in the overhead compartment.
A velvet drawstring bag
for his head, his most
delicate part, decapitated. He hates
the box. Imagine lying
nightly in your own coffin.
A vacant-jawed
cry. My fingertips roll
his eyes. *You're pathetic.*
He gets haircuts. He is silicone
and fibreglass, full of sputters
and spit. *This voice is shit. I need
a new voice.* You're fine,
I tell him, smoothing
his brow. You're fine.

PICTURE

While waiting for a letter, a failed attempt
to freeze the firmness of that porch with its No
Flyers plea, or the dizzy grip of hexagons on postwar
wallpaper. Lit screens recline, cooling their pained
portraits, staged polish, and deliberate mood.
Absent: the broken cobalt tone
of her voice, the jiggling blurry knee.

Scenes flip by without corners, stampless. A haze
evaporates outside the frame. An attempt to keep
the ultramarine day, the blue basin, the drip
of strangled rags. The white cutting board
must become something. I almost forgot your posy
heads, clustered in the garden, clutching dandelions
and kale. Lemon thickens. Light stuns the concrete,
the glass. All I remember is the lilac door, the scarlet
coverlet. A collar of unbleached linen. In colour,
an echo of what struck him.

A FEW ON SILENCE

1.

The cursor begs from the librarian's screen:
begin. A Boolean search delivers a flurry
of results. Coins won't release gumballs or floppy
disks from the machine beside the microfiche.
A pigeon considers a virtual likeness of his species.
All complaints are catalogued. The suggestion
box is empty, but locked.

2.

You keep all your secrets, don't you?
Are we being shy today?
Have you seen this person?
What happens now?
Did you feel it?
When will you know?
Did I hear voices?
How many of you are there?

3.

Even in quiet there is pretending
the cat's tail is a microphone. There is lying
together in an isolation booth while the insulated
panels do their thing. There are insular temperatures.
There is sitting on an amp so it won't up
and disappear. There is a fixed bandwidth, a wide berth
for the wrong words, the noisiest kinds of errors.

I MISS YOU

Tumbleweeds of fur float
to paralyzed mobiles. Goodwill
heel on its side. Cats guard
button jars, curate rock gardens,
alert to signals that flare in blank
door frames, warnings written
in static. Tails of patch
cords twitch over the banister.
A sink scrubbed with ocean,
cuts closed with salt, skin
rubbed pink. Happy veins.
Where snow was, a pumpkin
corpse. Muscles melt
at the still pressure of imagined
hands. The smooth spot of gum
where a tooth has been pulled.
A smile with a hole in it.

THE EXPLODING HOUSE

There were theories. Lazy with propane. A snarl of frayed wires. A hoard of aerosol cans. A careless séance. A husband, half-lit, who dealt in dynamite. They were the sort of couple who cooked meals like chicken with melted lemons. Foxes sucked on the tossed rinds. Everyone went to look when they heard the noise, cameras slung around their necks. None of them had ever been inside that house and now its contents surrounded them. A veil of pelts, hooked on high branches. Shingles and tiles, shuffled like cards, bobbed down the river. Her spoon collection—it rained spoons, very briefly. People pried them from the ground and examined the handles: Niagara Falls, Cape Breton, Maine. There were postcards, too: Wish You Were Here. Having a Gas in Las Vegas. A neighbour gathered the smashed snow globes and lined them up on her porch, careful not to cut her fingers. Everywhere she looked, something was out of place.

THEY WILL TAKE MY ISLAND

I squeezed everything I could from you,
sand escaping your collar, miniature horses
circling your sternum. You swung me
to sleep, then hollered all night
with the crows and the faucets.
I forgot my second-last home
under a blue net, was rescued
by nets and trapped by nets,
wrestled with rope, lifted silk
hauls of fish. I opened my arms.
I curled into nothing until I turned
into a shell. People forgive
themselves for more than this.
They will descend on roads
that hug the markets, charms
trembling from rearview mirrors.
They will crack the husks.
Like me, they will take what they can.

PROGRESS REPORT

We got sea monkeys in the mail from our moms.
We hosted cymbal recitals on the fire escape.
We explored cinemas still under construction.
We recalled every password and acronym.
We biked home drunk, avoiding statues and ponds.
We lamented the kissing skills of straight boys.
We developed vitamin and mineral deficiencies.
We considered stepping into oncoming traffic.
We flooded the basement and adopted a whale.
We packed our resumés with false qualifications.
We found the best pho, hidden in the suburbs.
We couldn't decide between chartreuse and pink.
We never knew for sure whether you meant it.
We left clues for those who would come after us.
We told terrible lies without meaning to.
We auditioned for spots at the trapeze academy.
We fashioned replicas of our childhood treehouse.
We placed ourselves in the paths of our enemies.
We questioned minor celebrities in waiting rooms.
We graphed our reactions and submitted them for review.

HAIRCUT

Nothing ever dries here
despite our glowing stoves.
Weak fan in the barbershop
hits dripping sausage curls. Soul mix
on the cassette player, silver moves
flashing over a slick cape. I call that
my crying block. No one likes a bag of hair
on their doorstep, but I didn't know how else
to tell you. Nine straight days of rain and I feel so clean.

JUST BE SIMPLE

I was knee deep in thistle, tasted blood
as pollen funnelled up from the earth.
I found an old stethoscope tossed in the lupins,
stitched a poncho for camouflage. There were people
sleeping in rows with ink on their hands. Waves have
removed transparency and danger from all shapes
of glass. I played dead, listed burials of favourite wells,
drew a blueprint for a raft, operated by pickup truck
science and lucky numbers. I lost all feeling in my right
side. I earned my lungs in a hearing contest, carried
my glasses in a sad case. All cliffs looked about to collapse.

ACCIDENTAL

Walk-up over a deli, next to the blinking lady's
silhouette. Every power failure she goes
to Bora Bora, comes back boasting new isotopes.
Left with wincing candles, we're ready with canned
water chestnuts, baby corn. We mourn the mood
light of the open refrigerator, hips clinking syrup
and film. Even the hidden businesses halt:
the speakeasy, the rub 'n' tug. Flash cards drift
from balconies. Earwigs nestled in pipes steel
themselves for flubs by the pianist who pounds
out blind scales, but false sharps never come.
She knows the notes by feel alone. We're forced
to hallucinate, to flood the room with gestures
no one can see: Come here. Closer. Stop.

RONNIE

robs the corner store. Or
tries to. I'm new, stocking
boxed tissues and eggs when
he busts in, striped ski mask,
requests cash
and cigarettes, half-
hearted index finger a toy
gun inside the kangaroo pouch
of his K-Way.
Mrs. MacLeod, calm as the milk
humming in its cool cube:
Ronnie, we know it's you.
Just go home and we'll forget
the whole thing.

Gives it another go
four days later. Same mask,
same stance, and I'm still
lining up and counting.
It's number three when
Mrs. MacLeod nudges the old
receiver between her shoulder
and chin, eyeing Ronnie, who eyes
her right back, arms slack,
waits while she slow rotary dials.
The cruiser offers no ceremony.
Not even a blurt of siren,
not even a silent
red and blue spin.

ELEPHANTS IN NEW BRUNSWICK

Favourite noun in your pocket picture dictionary,
columned with eagle, echo, earthquake. The texture
of flat illustrations showed you its skin
would be cool as clay. Your shoulders bound
by a seatbelt, hot buckle, air the taste of bleached
facecloths and mud. The petting-zoo brochure said local
creatures, but why not, in a land where station wagons sail
uphill in neutral and bridges have roofs and balloonists
land each fall? Why not when you've seen a car in a ditch,
a capsule burst into a pet in bathwater, the wisp of a moon
in daytime?

Big as a mascot, a triceratops, a starry radio tower.
You could stand on ten phone books and not manage
to cup its satellite-dish ears. You grow serious. The car
dips into small mountains. You feel the heartbeat, clang
of horseshoes ringing a stake. Wheels on gravel
are giftwrap tearing. In each surprise, something
you already know.

THINGS I'LL NEVER FORGET

A coat rack I'd marry. A baby toe in a cast. A tally of mild earaches. A ribeye at the boss's condo. A bathtub full of wigs. An unprofessional offer. A match struck on a chestnut. A coiffed and manicured June bug. An admonishment in translation. A severe antelope. A streetlight waiting for a bus.

A smell in the department. A catalogue of gossip. A limp, well-concealed. A stroke false alarm. A beautiful manoeuvre. A cuff on a sphygmomanometer. A vandalized Venn diagram. An issue with pigeons. A closet academic. An inappropriate venue. A critique of vaulted ceilings. A proposal during a fire drill.

A chorus of paper hats on my kitten's birthday. A crushed city followed by a pale snow. A philodendron pawned by a desperate custodian. A distant catastrophe tickling my bones. A pulse in the earth where a person once stood. A wound sutured with tinsel. A tiny fingernail that needs cutting, and nine more. A concave supper. A soundcheck at dawn.

INVALID

Onion halved on a counter,
twin rowboats rocking
beside a foggy blade.
The school bus empties,
gasping in the cold.
Calm in carrying small
bowls, in clean breaks
from archaic whims.
Lean over to unfasten
the day, wishes loosening,
a slowly popping catch.
Pair of stockings a tourniquet
on weeping pipes. Fever
persists, tunnels its way
through you, a blinding
compress. A touch, skating.
A litany of handles to let go.

THE RORSCHACH TEST IS IN

She saw hummingbirds in hot rooms,
their wings embroidered pink. Ice cream
looked like clouds to her, caves
like cotton. She was certain
she saw a man pouring gravy on the snow.

A pillar read over her shoulder.
The pills wore blank expressions.
She closed her hand around a piece
of technology, concluded umbrellas
were the core of this community.

She saw Jesus in a bowl
of cling peaches, glazed and kind.
She saw a town in a typeface.
Her wrists were as ugly as yams.
Her yawn was glue. The days passed
so slowly, she could hardly believe it.

BAD DAY

You lived on Timbits and tap
water, coffee competing with
zoplicone. Maybe it was the food,
instant potato, or those mild
seizures under microwaved
blankets, but your face was the blankest
part of you. Your shadow smoked
on the brown lawn. Non-ironic
t-shirt logo (your dad's construction
company, and you worked there). We paired
suits to kill hours, predicted the next punch-
line on *Friends*. High odds of repeat
episodes. When they refused you
the key to the shower. Hell-bent on
Halloween. Nurse as warlock, makeup
and cloak, sprinkled cheap candy
on wilted sheets. We tore at the sugar,
our gowns. A taste like sucking on
a menthol penny, a headache, a
nap. You won't remember anything
I said. A hurricane happened
and we didn't notice, cozy generators,
flowing currents, trees' roots
pointed at the sky.

THINK ABOUT BUOYANCY

Call the coast guard. A seal is stuck
to the ice. He's certainly not just sitting.
I held a vigil from shore as the ships
conspired to unleash themselves. I could
believe each thing was a disaster, first frost
a distress signal. Send a dinghy, a helicopter,
or at least a life jacket, lobbed out a trap
door. No fingertips necessary. Cast a string
of buoys. Upset a bucket of bright cones.

I could believe each thing was a disaster.
The man tapping at my door, ocean breath,
requesting that I make him a cup of tea.
Rimless frames, pool of water over each eye.
On red-letter days, head count in the elevator.
We rolled paper lips in the big outside world,
watched the flat harbour until the leader
in the lanyard yelled, *Allons-y!* Language
of herds, orders towards wellness.

Each person was given an axe, a parking
meter, a metronome, a locket, and an oatcake
and told, *Make a shelter. Think about gravity,*
they suggested. *Think about buoyancy, the force
of liquid on bobbing objects, a duck in the tub.*
We hammered without manuals, added
flourishes: swan planters, a painted mural. In
the end, we were never rescued. Gulls picked
at the scraps of clothing placed to spell SOS,
a plea shredded and reconsidered.

FIGHT OR FLIGHT

After a tense breakfast of crystallized jam,
he ran hard as he could over an iron
bridge, racing the shutdown of nonessential
systems. Loons blared into a blank sky.
The husk of his self remained seated
at the table, facing the steamrolled globe
on his placemat, spooning oats and braced
for the body's dominoes. The swelling planets
of his pupils. Running hard, hard not to see
the hypothetical burglar or bear, real paws
or leather gloves, toppled rations or firework
of glass. Sure of spies skunking around
behind ferns or paper fans. His husk
put his face on the table. Branches shrugged
above him, the nervous systems of trees
a feat of engineering. His husk listened
to the pianist in the next room, imaginary
wire taut from the top of her skull
to the ceiling, ballet posture. Rain
of felted mallets. One explosion
detonates another.

PARACHUTE

A garage band soundchecks
in the garage. Orange clouds
and I was tricked indoors to
see a dove, burbling in its cage.

Hands hold wire as a string
breaks, faint curses. Streamers
stained with footprints, cracked
cans litter a hammock. A falling
out could occur at any moment.
Moths swim to red lanterns.

There are too many people here.
The crowd rises in the house
like a tide, begins to use windows
as exits. They don't believe
they can fly, only hope their paths
will be slow, their landings soft.

NOTES & ACKNOWLEDGEMENTS

The title "Stranger at the Wake" is courtesy of Al Tuck.

The shark in a jar belongs to Andrew Lee.

The image "eyes large as teacups" in "Bakery Tale" is from Hans Christian Anderson's fairytale "The Tinder Box."

Some of the phrases about colour in "Picture" are pulled from Vincent Van Gogh's letters to his brother, Theo.

"Just Be Simple" is the name of a song by Songs: Ohia.

Ronnie's failed robberies took place in Sydney, Nova Scotia.

"Elephants in New Brunswick" is for my sister, Megan.

In "Think About Buoyancy," the call to the Coast Guard is from a story told by my dad.

Earlier versions of some of these poems have appeared in *The Antigonish Review, Carousel, The New Quarterly, This Magazine, The Puritan, The Coast,* and Paul Vermeersch's online poetry project, *They Will Take My Island.* Many thanks to the respective editors.

I am grateful to the Ontario Arts Council for financial support through the Writers' Reserve Program.

I am indebted to the students and faculty of the University of Guelph's Creative Writing MFA program, for their friendship and encouragement. Thank you to members of The Common, to Erica Butler, Stephanie Johns, and Chantal Tardiff for patiently listening to poems on an island while surrounded by docile wild dogs, to Jeff Latosik, and to Paul Hammond. Thanks to Kevin Munhall at

Queen's University for poet-friendly employment. Thanks to my family and friends.

Thanks to Denis De Klerck at Mansfield Press, and to Stuart Ross, dream editor—this book wouldn't exist without him.

Thank you especially to Lachie, for infinite things big and small, every day, with all of my heart.

Jaime Forsythe is a poet, fiction writer, editor, and journalist. Her work has appeared in a number of magazines and journals, including *This Magazine*, *Geist*, and *The New Quarterly*. She is a regular arts contributor to *The Coast*, and the editor of the fiction anthology *Transits* (Invisible Publishing). A graduate of the University of Guelph's Creative Writing MFA program, she lives in Halifax, Nova Scotia.

OTHER BOOKS FROM MANSFIELD PRESS

Poetry

Nelson Ball, *In This Thin Rain*
Stephen Brockwell & Stuart Ross, eds., *Rogue Stimulus: The Stephen Harper Holiday Anthology for a Prorogued Parliament*
Alice Burdick, *Holler*
Gary Michael Dault, *The Milk of Birds*
Pier Giorgio Di Cicco, *Early Works*
Christopher Doda, *Aesthetics Lesson*
Rishma Dunlop, *Lover Through Departure: New and Selected Poems*
Jason Heroux, *Emergency Hallelujah*
David W. McFadden, *What's the Score?*
Leigh Nash, *Goodbye, Ukulele*
Lillian Necakov, *Hooligans*
Peter Norman, *At the Gates of the Theme Park*
Natasha Nuhanovic, *Stray Dog Embassy*
Catherine Owen & Joe Rosenblatt, with Karen Moe, *Dog*
Jim Smith, *Back Off, Assassin! New & Selected Poems*
Robert Earl Stewart, *Campfire Radio Rhapsody*
Carey Toane, *The Crystal Palace*
Priscila Uppal, *Winter Sport: Poems*
Steve Venright, *Floors of Enduring Beauty*

Fiction

Marianne Apostolides, *The Lucky Child*
Kent Nussey, *A Love Supreme*
Marko Sijan, *Mongrel*
Tom Walmsley, *Dog Eat Rat*

Non-Fiction

George Bowering, *How I Wrote Certain of My Books*
Pier Giorgio Di Cicco, *Municipal Mind*
Amy Lavender Harris, *Imagining Toronto*

For a complete list of Mansfield Press titles, please visit mansfieldpress.net